When I Speak To the Dead

By: Chad Smith

Every word in this book was written by me. No AI was used for ideas or editing.
This comes from the heart.

To find more books by me visit:

www.gattaca.world

S

Staten House

And those that haunt me

will you ever fade?

will you always breathe?

cold thoughts?

into me?

as I sleep?

This collection is dedicated to my Aunt Linda. I miss you.

And the ghost of my dead brother.

"a song ends, and dark begins—
dear sip, dear shotgun, dear pound,
the party flips its switches down."

- Hummel, Maria. "Letter to My Blackout." Letter to My Blackout by Maria Hummel, https://www.poetryfoundation.org/poetrymagazine/poems/150043/letter-to-my-blackout. Accessed 26 Feb. 2024.

"I could hear my heart beating. I could hear everyone's heart. I could hear the human noise we sat there making, not one of us moving, not even when the room went dark."

- Carver, Raymond, author. "What We Talk About When We Talk About Love.", by Knopf, 1981.

"I'm haunted by all
the space that I
will live without
you."

- Richard Brautigan

"You should focus more on the living, skinny human."

- Kalfar, Jarosla, author. "Spaceman of Bohemia.", by Little, Brown and Company, 2017.

table of contents

This is a warning for you, dear reader,
as it was for me.

Out here on the boundaries,
talking to ghosts.

This is going to hurt.

"I sure hope that old lady was wrong about death not being the end of it."

"After You've Gone." True Detective, created by Nic Pizzolatto, Season 1, Episode 7, Home Box Office, Inc., 2014.

I.

In the Land of Dead Unicorns (Part 1)

They wash up onto the beach
pink   and   white   fading
     Horns driven into the sand by the surf
         eyes pale and white

Driven from a faraway island
     some are missing legs
     some are missing their manes
     some bloated and some still dying
Heaving their last breaths
     as jellyfish wash onto the shore to join them

Once they were majestic
     flowing in the wind
         shining in the sun

Now they just rot
     picked apart by seagulls.

To My Aunt

I wonder
about strangers who smile,
and I don't know if
you are watching me
or if you visited me
today
though I felt you move
through my books of Wonder
reading the lines as if
they were but sparkles
in your imagination.

I slept through dreams
and you told me
this was coming,
and I closed my eyes
afraid of the morning,
afraid of a tomorrow without
you.

Your mind was always moving
in places I could never go,
landscapes you dreamt of with Coleridge.
I only ask that you sing
soft hymns in the night.

37 Minutes After Your Funeral

I stood on the bathroom tile
looking at the dirty bathtub
and cheap cosmetics,
trying to find a solace
from your empty spaces.

Silas Marner stands open
on the back of the toilet
to the last page of
the thirteenth chapter.

The number still scares me.

Maybe if you had slipped past
this unlucky chapter,
you would still be standing
in front of the stove,
instead of falling with awkward grace
into my silent arms.

Eating Oranges

"There sat I, a faded being, under faded leaves."

- Franz Kafka

I keep thinking we buried you alive,
that you're moving around down there,
pleading with me for help.

A small lizard glares at me
as it crawls out from under
a green leaf to lie on the warming sidewalk.

The morning bird's early song
dances off my eardrums
like the magic of your voice.

I want to go pick oranges
and sit under the trees and eat them,
my fingers peeling back the orange flesh,
the juice running down my arms.
But I can still see you
under those trees.

There

I was at your house the night
your brother died
He had gone upstairs
to take a shower

We were drinking red wine
with your neighbors
And talking about the nature
of consciousness

I had told a terrible joke
that everyone laughed at

When we heard the sound
We sat there frozen
Afraid
Afraid to move

Before, when people were talking all around me
I thought I heard him weeping
but then realized it was water in the pipes

until we heard the sound.

Whence Came My Darkness

Rain blew across my mind,
as I watched you from my car window,
sitting in a swing, staring at your little feet.

And I drove home into my world
of an empty house and
a colorful Netflix show,
away from books and old chalkboards,
and the thirsty mouths
open in embrace
yearning for recess.

How could I ever have known I would find you
hours later
hanging from the swing set
the chain digging into your soft neck
giving you the freedom you always wanted.

Stadium Lights

I walked down Culver street,
fading in the mahogany dusk
towards Lincoln Park ballfield.
It seems so far away now,
and my legs ache more with every step.

Stepping into the park,
the chipped green stadium seats
surround me with their sadness.
The hard roughness digs
into my bones as I sit down.

It's been 52 years since
I played this game,
stood on the mound,
facing down the batter.
I memorized the steps
as I walked from home to the mound.

The great distance.

Looking out there now,
I can almost see the batter in his stance
can almost hear
the sound of the ball as it slides past
his swing into the mitt.

I used to pat the rosin bag in my hand,
and let the chalk float into my nose,
it reminded me of cleaning
the erasers in Elementary school.

Sometimes, I still hold my old glove
up to my face and inhale deeply,
the musky stink of sweat and leather

fills me like stadium lights
on a warm spring night.

I can't forget those smells,
the clean, clipped grass
the fresh, brown dirt on the mound,
popcorn and hotdogs as
the fans slowly fill the stadium.

Tonight, the memories shimmer
through me like falling asleep
in front of a flickering television.
So many faces, so long ago,
I can still see them...
in the twilight of my life.

Door

When I was young
the Bible told me
Behold
god stands at the door and knocks
would I let him in?

Now I am older
casting my lot into
the dark waters
I feel alone

And I hear no one knocking.

But if I were to find **your** door
and knock

would *you let me in?*

Building

I make these plans
every day
of this perfect world
we will build with Legos.

A red city
your favorite color
with people all over
riding cars and trains
and a mountain in the middle
holding a giant who will
protect us all.

But as every day passes
we don't see each other
and no red blocks
form a wall.

Day by day
the map in my head fades,
the cars disappear,
the trains stop rolling down the tracks
the city crumbles
the blocks fall
red, blue, green, yellow
all lost...

II.

In the Land of Dead Unicorns (Part 2)

As they wash back out

into the sea

their horns gleam

off the sky

    off the sun

one last farewell.

the green waves

    and white foam

    over them.

When you were still here

I loved tucking you in at night
your dark hair was always so perfect
you always   brushed it   before bedtime

You loved to snuggle against your pillow
and I would read you stories

      about

raindrops and bubblegum

But when I stared at you
      in your tiny casket

      all I could think of was

              rain

in front yards made of sand

I used to see you
      at parties on the beach

a fragile
      trembling
           ghost

at the edge
      of the crowd

at a surging
      music festival
           in the middle of July

getting out of a car
      at RaceTrac
           in orange October leaves

always
      your mouth
           whispering
                words

I could not understand

I traveled to a white sand beach
      in Mykonos

and held giant pink shells
      to my ear

silence.

collapsing

i remember going to see you
in the middle of the night
to watch you unwind
to buy some time
but the nightmare goes on
standing out here

the moon
wanes on to every last breath
of the dying night
casting its last glowing embers
on the sidewalk of an empty street

downcast yellow lights from a passing car
echo on my eyelids closed in prayer
in this golden globe as I lose hope
that crashes to the tile floor
of your hospital room.

On the Turn

two years
     you've
          been gone

interesting
     that on this day

in the midst of
     our drought
          grass so dry
               it crackles black

the rain
     comes

these blue winds
     blowing cold
          air across
               me

that night
     so many
          years ago

we hit that turn
     coming down
          White Oak Mountain

too hard right
     you skidded

and we both almost

left

on the turn.

the blood
of my ancestors

pour
off in these glasses.

sp few left now
so many
lie
broken
on the floor.

I wonder
what they are trying
to say.

III.

In the Land of Dead Unicorns (Part 3)

You were **always**
  dying
      and screaming

but this time
  maybe

the unicorns are all gone now
their brightness faded from the world
the pink and blue
      all grey

I walk through the sand
  hoping to find something
      but feel nothing

for the first time
  in a lifetime
you say kind things
  you love me
    and you are proud of me
        engraved on a cheap watch

and I keep walking
  through the sand
    feeling nothing.

Dear Mr. Henry

I'm worried. Your words are scaring me more than they ever have. For the first time, I feel like I'm losing control. I'm losing the ability to discern reality I think. I simply don't know what to do.

Dear Mr. Henry:

My words to you have been coming less and less. I'm running in a direction with no place to stop. I feel this blinding pain at night...deeply

Dear Mr. Henry:

That last night, when we were drinking at the Trink bar, afterwards when we were walking down the street. I could have sworn I saw a light flicking around your shoulders.

Dear Mr. Henry:

Oh I'm sad today...your continued lack of words hurt me. "Nothing haunts like silence" I think you once said. I'm looking out my window, watching pretty girls walk down the street. One in particular catches my eye...she has long red hair flowing down out of her coat. I can't see her face, it's obscured by her green and blue scarf...but I'm certain she is beautiful.

I miss the brightness of you...

Glow

I wonder
and I linger

pause

waiting for the moment
you step into the room

I wait for the time
when I see you next...

and I am surprised
when I turn around and see you

standing there
head slightly tilted
a smile playing upon your lips
and light dancing in eyes
so filled with thought.

And I had been planning
so much I wanted to tell you
so many words to say

but the room is glowing now
the room is changing
and I can't find my words
because all I see is you.

How Did You Fit All That Hate In Your Heart?

I miss you sometimes
on these golden kiss fall mornings,
we were better at being kids
sneaking a beer under your parent's back porch.

I can't remember all the things we did
the dew mornings we spent by the lake,
watching the early morning trout fishermen
cast their lines from their boat.

We were walking down Broadway in the fall,
our breath icy in the air
sweet with the fragrant musk of dying leaves,
you pulled your fur collar tighter around your neck,
and I knew you were fading away.

But my forgotten dreams
sitting on that stone bench with me all night
hoping you would move a little closer,
some sign that the jagged bolts in my stomach
were not mine alone.

no more happy endings

remember when forever meant
a really long time,
those lost fragments of memory
like blue skies looking up at you

everything you ever cared about,
those sacrifices that broke your tears
and sucked your heart into mine.

I tear myself in two

      every time I look at you

every time a girl passes me

      on the street wearing your perfume

every time I find a strand

      of your long blonde hair
      floating in the air of my cold house

every time my radio sings blue songs

      you used to sing to me when
      I couldn't find sleep

every time October breaks

and the leaves fall in death
bleeding red and orange

I remember you dancing in the wind

filling your arms with leaves
breaking my heart

The New One

He has a new album coming out

      our favorite guy

I think you would have liked IT

You would have called me

  and we would have talked so much

ending up with 'When the Tygers Broke Free'

      your favorite Pink Floyd song

We would have had a listening party at your house

just you and me

      an excuse to drink some whiskey

          and listen to those sad Gilmour notes

he's playing the standup again

but now it's just me

   wishing you were here.

IV.

In the Land of Dead Unicorns (Part 4)

remnants
      pieces

once again
      floating into the
            white
                  sand

We walk down the beach
you so happy
      your red golden retriever floof
          blowing into the wind

Once when there were more
      you were so afraid

You find a piece of a neck
mane
      grey in the surf
         and fling it
            with all your might.

Savannah

And her name makes me think
of a girl with golden hair
flowing down towards the ground
walking along the quiet streets.

Her murder haunts
the historic district like a
grey shadow from Bonaventure
looking for contemplation with god.

And the bird lady holds her arms up
as an eternal shrug
in the cemetery where the weeping willows
lament the tombstones older than time,
indifferent to Minerva stealing dirt
from a lawyer's grave.

Savannah, with her casual ways
and to-go cups full of wine
she graces the back shadows of my mind.

While on River Street, T-shirt tourists
bump into one another on the cobble stone streets
I am in the park on a wooden bench
writing this for you.

Of Playgrounds and Cages

I watch him pace
      circles
            around the cage

eyes staring
      so focused
looking out towards memories
      a future
            he cannot see.

The tiger pacing his cage in a country zoo
      round and round
eyes focused on something far away

And suddenly I am back
      on a gravel playground
staring at the fence
      looking out at the green fields

full of yellow daisies

beyond my reach.

And I wonder
if I am doing the same

      pacing my own cage
eyes fuzzy
      focused on something I cannot see.

When My Fragile Wings Would Shiver

we drink so much now
living our lives somewhere between
our dark oak bar and the wind swept streets

do you hear anything
when the lights go out?
have you lost the feeling you had?
the one that buzzed in you
told you that you could do something
with your life
that you could make a difference
in these kids' lives
the ones you stand in front of every day

they give you empty looks
and once you tried to fill them up
but now you look right through them

and my fragile wings still shiver
when I think of you
knowing your light is burning out
long before your youth takes flight.

The ceiling fan

At my uncle's house
his spare bedroom
was musty and sweet

With green velvet curtains
the ceiling fan
whined
and wobbled

and told me things about
      my future

I didn't want to believe

Micks

I can almost feel my father
sitting at this table,
in faded blue jeans and T-shirt
as young as I am now
in Micks, on the day
after Christmas in 1974,
waiting for my mother
sick with blood poisoning
to give birth to twins,
not knowing that only one
would survive the violence
on the twenty-seventh.

Today, I'm the one watching
the rain drizzle outside,
and I don't know if he'll survive
this birth of cancer,
his personality fading every day.

I look up into the sky
as cloudy as it was on
the day before my birth,
and I only hope that tomorrow
isn't as grey as it was for you
all those years ago.

V.

In the Land of Dead Unicorns (Part 5)

The heat

      we

            set records

                  every day.

Everything seems
      to be dying.

Rain
      a memory of the past.

We go out into the surf
      warm as a hot bath

holding hands

looking for them
      are there any left?

A matted clump of hair
      washes
            over my feet.

I don't know

      from
            what beast

it fell from.

So many bright
      dead things

once floated here

all those years ago.

My Twin Brother

Today I am wearing yellow
and I stand in Greenwood, SC
at your tiny, heart-shaped tombstone.
You died on your birthday.

Yesterday, I felt alone
stripped of everything, I was lost.
I reached out for a connection
staring into the sky
looking for some sign of you.

Today, my feet sink in this mud,
and my hand grips a single daisy.
I haven't seen you in so many years,
and I can't remember you.
It was too dark in our mother's womb.

My hand opens slowly
like a preacher reaching out
to grasp his congregation.
The flower rolls and falls
bouncing once on your little
before hitting the mud.

Unicorns at the Lake

I went back

    to that old house

        we had by the lake

with its black water

    and red muddy banks

the door was caved in

most of the windows

gone

I went into your old room

    where you breathed as a baby

the pink unicorn wallpaper

    torn

        peeling

        I trembled.

The Birds Cry

sometimes they fall from the sky
and I don't want to listen
I don't know why

maybe they are reminding us
of an end that we don't want
to think about

flying, soaring into the white clouds
      surrounded by blue

I wonder if they just give up
tired
     and fall.

Forgetting How To Listen

"But two weeks later he killed her. Of course."

- Mike
- "Half Measures." Breaking Bad, created by Vince Gilligan, season 3, episode 12, Sony Pictures Television, 2010.

You have to go
      but he can be sweet

You have to go
      but I don't want him to be alone

You have to go
      but sometimes he doesn't hit me

You have to go
      but he brings me flowers

You have to go
      but he owns so many guns

You have to go
      but he cut back on his drinking

You have to go
      but you won't

                until you're gone.

The man standing outside Dunkin' Donuts when I was 23

He rants

    and yells

        CHARLIE!!!!

wearing full camouflage

and screams at someone
who isn't there

he has a paper cup

Christian and I go down for coffee
    again

        he yells at the invisible enemy

          I laugh

Christian says

"That man probably saw horrors we will never see. And here we are

    shitting on his grave."

dark blurs

like a tunnel
      waking up
            in a dark
                   hotel
                       room

where am I?

the microwave clocks
      says

0:15
      in green

I hear a scream
      my aunt stands
            over me
                 with my mother

in the dark

I walk out of the bed
      into the hallway
            still dark

and bump into
      something

off in the distance

wood
splinters against

dark skies

I am so scared

of the dark now.

Hyperactive

For some reason
I think of red and green Christmas lights
from that night
even though it was mid-summer

I remember sweating
on the side of the road

unable to catch my breath

People tried to talk to me
I couldn't understand the words

It was cold
I remember looking at my breath
wondering why it was so cold

People tried to talk to me
I couldn't hear them

Watching you be loaded
into the ambulance
I couldn't see your face

People tried to talk to me

I couldn't understand

My Son Climbs In

beside me, falls asleep
in a lump, all his jump

and shimmy
run out. He's about

as wide and as deep
as a pillow, plumped.

And I...propped
slumped and reading,

needing no one to
tuck me in, needing

nothing, really...
eventually I take

to nodding, nodding
with all I know

and have known
toward the unknown.

Later, I wake,

my book in my lap,
the lamp still bright,

to find him grinding
his tiny white teeth

with all his might.

The Wallpaper

says hello
The wallpaper
misses you something
awful.

The wallpaper
can't stop wondering when
you were thinking of
coming home.

The clock's
moved on.

The sink's ten
million tears
are dry.

Our floors have gotten
over you, or so they
claim
and claim.

The windows
clearly feel the same.

But call me.

Call me
soon, my love,
and tell me
what to say

the next time
the fading and

tedious
wallpaper
whispers your name.

Field of Rain

I hid here as a child
and watched you pace
in your cotton white dress,
barely a year older than me.
Back and forth you would go,
screaming and yanking at your hair,
mimicking the things your father
did to you at home.

The trees stopped growing
in this open meadow where we played.
Surrounded by thick trees we felt alone
and safe from the grown-ups.

This was our field.

The grass feels thick,
and the leaves still look the same,
but now I am so out of place here.
Now I'm the one who's alone
with a child as crazy as you were.

But I cannot find the solace
you seemed to find here.
The grey clouds touch and thunder,
and I turn and walk out into
your field.

Brother

When I speak to the dead

i was screaming
i must have been terrified
coming into this world
with the cold corpse of my brother
into the arms of a confused mother
and passionless father...

i must have kept screaming
he was gone along with the warmth
we had lived in for nine months
gone forever...

i must be screaming now
though my mouth is closed
and no one can hear me
unless he raises his ear
to my fragile voice.

For Karen

your classes were sometimes magic

I was in my Stephen King phase
and would try to freak you out
with poems about other worlds and blood.

I never could.

You always just told me how to make them
better.

and you saw through
all my teenage bullshit.

how I wish
      you were still around

You would have helped me
      make all of this better.

A few times

I heard your voice
       telling me to do things
usually killing

      plants

once or more
all those years ago

I saw you standing in the garden
       in the trail
between the rows of wine grapes

you always were in a world of trembles

I knew you weren't there

      but I felt you

        and as I walked forward

             ice.

Still Afraid of Ghosts

this
          night
we
          were
                    sitting

by
          the
                    pool

remembering
                    you

you walked
          by
                    me

Hey buddy

your smile

that grin

I stopped
          breathing

cold

and you were gone

          again.

Untitled (the last thing I will write for you Aunt Linda)

through the fields we ran

tall wheat grass

    green and brown

        blowing against our bare legs

my aunt says she feels empty

    trapped in a hollow life

        smoking cigarettes and playing solitaire

with dirty red and white cards

    corners broken and bent

and we ran laughing

    as if there was no tomorrow.

where is this taking me

we were coming back
            weren't we
                        from a dive
                                    in Key West

we stopped to eat
            enormous amounts
                        of shrimp and conch

looking at the green and yellow
            houses on stilts
                        and boats
                                    tied off at the docks.

I think about the names
            she called you, my father

and
            (Don't you dare talk about that!)

how mean
            she became
                        in the end

how mean
            she always was

maybe
            that is why you
                        denied

every

one

of her dying wishes

maybe

maybe.

The cold white tile

On the hospital floor again
      I sink
            further in

and feel the cold
      I wonder if anyone has died in this spot

outside

a man is screaming for a blanket

my half-closed lids
gaze out across the floor

to the door closed

I

      shiver
           tremble
               quake
                  and smile

I close my eyes
      and fall into a dreamless sleep

but then dream

Of a shiny black night
driving up a grey gravel driveway
I am the passenger
the house is bathed in blue lights
and dark iron gates hover

before

me

and the floor again
        someone is speaking

The nurse who loves me
rubs my shoulders
I crawl to my knees and she helps me
back into bed.

She injects something into my IV

and I fall

        fall

                fall

cold air

Scared of night Mares

Thy rod and thy staff
they no longer comfort me

I cannot move

my favorite uncle
          dying
                    in hospice

liquid morphine
          squirted on his gums
                    every four hours

wakes up and hugs me

          with rage

anger that he's dying.

this life don't mean shit
          he says.

later in the night
          his wife

          crawls out of a dark
                    mouth

                              cave

jaw melting
          screaming
                    mewing
undulations

weeks later
       I watch dirt
              thrown
                     onto his casket.

The mare
       all black
              against
                     a sky of ink.

I cannot move.

I exhale into cold air.

"I have taken from you
       the next one will hurt
              the most.

But I ride
       in the darkness

       feel
              the rush of
                   my body

see my breath
       hot in the air

I ride for you."

At   17

You looked so small

curled up in your hospital bed

    asleep

we were waiting for the video call

the psych call

    to get you out of the ER

        and into the psych facility

    you were so sleepy

    from your suicide attempt

You looked so small

I remembered you as this little blonde-haired child

    so happy

        on a big pillow

You looked so small.

In the Land of Dead Unicorns (Part 6)

so far gone
        (glimpses)
now

our children's children
        no longer believe

they laugh
        at us
            the few who
                remain

we remember the rumors
        of happiness
            on an island
                far away

and when they
        finally
arrived

we couldn't believe the news

        but the smell
            miles from the beach

of a million hearts
        breaking at once.

there was no denying

        even still

the sight from
        the boardwalk
            into the white sand.

so much ruin
        beautiful

            in death.

Epilogue

The stars burn like pieces of glass cut from the sun

Acknowledgments

This book would not have happened without the encouragement of my wife Amiee and my kid Anastasia Smith. Bryan and Andrew, I hope you never tire of reading my stuff. I love all of you.

Cover art by Chad and Amiee Smith

About the Author

Chad Smith is a consultant and author hiding out in the Caribbean. He is married and lives with two neurotic golden retrievers.

www.ingramcontent.com/pod-product-compliance
Lightning Source LLC
Chambersburg PA
CBHW022045170626
46808CB00003B/1368